JIM RUZICKA: ETIO... KIL...

MW00352375

Copyright © 2022 by Anthony Meoli - Meoli Forensic Consulting, LLC

All rights reserved. No part of this book may be reproduced, distributed, or transmitted in any form or by any means, including photocopying, recording, or other electronic or mechanical methods, without the prior written permission of the author.

First Edition 1 2 3 4 5 6 7 8 9 10

ISBN: 978-1-66787-333-6

Foreword

My name is Jim Ruzicka. I have been asked why I raped women and committed murders as a young person. No one cared, as usual; they just categorized me and locked me up. Forty-eight years later, I still cannot honestly say why I did the things I did.

Maybe it was hate, anger, revenge, thinking I was getting back at the men and women who had abused me as a kid. I was afraid and ashamed of what I did and thought I could hide it all so no one would know what I had done. What I was really doing was trying to hide from myself and blame others for everything I did. The truth, even though I didn't know it then, is that I had a choice of the road I went down. The treatment I received as a kid did play a part in everything, that much is true, but I still made that choice. As the good Lord knows, I regret what I did and the two lives I took. If I could give up my life this second to bring my victims back to life, I would.

3

I am in prison and have been for more than forty-eight years. I will die here I know, alone and forgotten. I chose to change and better myself as a person rather than let the prison turn me into an animal. No one has to pity or condemn me further; I condemn myself each and every day. I cannot change the past, even though I pray I could. I am not really religious, but I have asked the Lord for forgiveness and to watch over the two souls whose physical lives I took. I am more remorseful and regretful for what I did than words alone can ever express. What I did, I did. I am not going to sugarcoat it.

This is my story, good and bad. I ask for no pity for my memories, as I lay my life before you. You will see me either as a demon or a changed man, but I will know the remorse I feel is real and not just words to placate others.

—Jim Ruzicka

My victims:

Nancy Pauline Kinghammer, Seattle, Washington, age sixteen. (February 23, 1957 – February 15, 1974)

Penny Marie Haddenham, Seattle, Washington, age fifteen. (November 19, 1958 – February 21, 1974)

Introduction

I first began corresponding with James Edward Ruzicka in late 2016. What began as a sporadic relationship in 2016 soon blossomed into weekly contact via written correspondence in 2017. Telephonic communications began in the latter stages of 2017. To put the written relationship into numerical perspective, from May 2017 to December 2017, I received more than twenty-nine letters and several drawings. Each letter averaged about three to four pages, which was slightly higher than most inmates who write one to two pages. The combination of time and trust led to 2018 being the breakthrough year, and I began to learn why he committed multiple sexual assaults and two murders.

As a board-certified clinical counselor, I know that reliving trauma can be difficult for anyone. Patience, time, and trust are needed to break through the human mask. We all have masks, how we wear them is our own choice. One of the biggest misconceptions about serial killers—defined as two or more killings with a latent period (cooling off) between each murder or murders—is that all of them lack remorse. This is untrue. How and why they lacked remorse at the time of the crimes is really what needs further exploration.

As time goes by, nearly every serial killer has some degree of remorse. It might not resemble the remorse that we think of as normal, but it is there. To put it simply, in my professional and clinical opinion, it is more likely that serial killers have a deeply muted sense of remorse rather than no remorse at all.

The reason many experts and academics see serial killers as completely lacking in remorse is that the depravity of their crimes does not fit within societal norms. Most do not spend years getting to know their subjects, rather they do simple tests like mental status exams— cursory outward-perception examination by the clinician, which often change from day to day, week to week, or month to month on every patient. Their acts, which are often dark and depraved, are just not thought of as human in nature. The mind thinks that anyone with an ounce of feeling for another human being would not do such a thing, so, clearly, they lack remorse. That is the easy way to think. That is the simple way to think. That is also a terrible way to understand why someone committed the acts they did to another human being. It takes time to understand the why and getting to know the why is what I specialize in doing.

It is not a pleasant experience; it has its own repercussions, including increased blood pressure, lack of sleep, dark thoughts, imagining the crime scenes over and over again, re-traumatizing myself with getting the facts straight, looking at the victims' faces over and over — all of which I have to live with to create my interviews and books. But without deeply immersing myself into who the killer was and who they are now, I will never get to know the why. One might argue this is just research, but it is far different when you are fielding dozens of phone calls, emails, and letters every month for nearly three decades. To say it does not weigh on me would be a lie. It does.

The very fact that most homicides, in fact more than 80 percent of all homicides, involve people known to the victim or have engaged with the victim in some capacity, tells us that acting out against a stranger is something we need to understand more simply because it is relatively rare. Given that most serial killers choose random victims who are unrelated to them in any way might lead to speculative notions. Some of these notions include the idea that this is done to escape detection, to avoid making an obvious pattern, or to perpetrate their crimes longer before detection. This is again the obvious choice, something to presume if a researcher does not take the time to get to know the killer's intent on a more intimate level.

What separated Jim Ruzicka from other serial killers was how quickly he responded to my inquiries. At the time we began to communicate, Ruzicka had already served forty-two years in prison. Simply put, Jim Ruzicka is one of the longest-living incarcerated serial killers in the United States. He is the single oldest serial killer (seventy-two years old as of this writing) in the state of Washington, now in his forty-eighth year of incarceration.

To give this historic perspective, the infamous Hillside Strangler cases in California and Washington took place nearly a half decade after Ruzicka's crimes. Oddly enough, Kenneth Bianchi, one of the two convicted Hillside Stranglers, would eventually be imprisoned in the very same pod as Jim Ruzicka for almost eight years when he was at Walla Walla State Prison. In a way, his age and personality traits greatly helped with this interview because he operates more openly with traditional communication. While email was certainly a tool that facilitated the

10

clarification of some of the finer details when completing this interview, it was not the main method used.

Jim Ruzicka has been remorseful for his actions for many decades. Why he committed his crimes comes back to what I have spoken about for years at forensic seminars and conferences, and to college students across the country. It is my belief that violence is a learned trait, but more so in that when an individual encounters these four particular traits, he or she is more prone to committing violence against others. I call this *Quadrant Theory.* The *Quadrant Theory of Predictive Violence* to be more specific. *Quadrant Theory* means that the individual will have suffered from *abuse, neglect, abandonment, and anger.*

This theory is based on decades of actual experience with serial killers, murderers, arsonists, serial snipers, and bank robbers who answered my letters, spoke with me over the phone, allowed me to visit in prison, or emailed me the finer details of their lives before they committed violence against others. The data that I have compiled from their collective backgrounds showed that more than 90 percent of these killers had at least three of the quadrant principles present. In most cases, all four traits were present in some form. When taken together, it was noted that most of the men and women who were contacted could be broken down as suffering from extensive trauma related to these four major categories. Anger was present in every single case of serial murder. Murder, in its truest form, is the ultimate act of human anger and emotion. Even when murder is committed without malice aforethought (premeditation), the final act is one of vengeance, revenge, or the thought that one is getting even.

The first trait of *Quadrant Theory* is abuse. Jim Ruzicka's childhood abuse was severe, prolonged, and repetitive, and was psychological, sexual, and physical in its manifestation.

First, as it relates to abuse, were numerous losses in his life. While one would not immediately jump to abuse with childhood loss, Ruzicka learned that half of his ten brothers and sisters had died before he had reached the age of six. Ruzicka was told he was "no good," and that he could never live up to the expectations of his mother.

Loss early in life is extremely traumatic and needs to be processed. Jim Ruzicka was never afforded any counseling, and his mother continued to have children, almost immediately after losing each one to illness or under mysterious circumstances. When Jim was six years old, he learned that his closest sibling, Linda, needed to go to the hospital for a heart operation. Ruzicka was upset at the thought of losing his emotionally closest sister but went with his mother and step-father to the hospital. Ruzicka remembers listening to the doctors and nurses, and although very young, he knew things were not looking good. He begged to be allowed to see her, but they ignored his requests. Finally, risking his own life, he snuck through a window and climbed onto the third-floor ledge of the building just to see into her room. It was not until nurses at the Children's Orthopedic Hospital in Seattle, Washington, saw him that security was notified. Security grabbed him and brought him back to his parents. When they got home, Jim was savagely beaten by both of his parents for being so irresponsible. His sister, Linda Marie Wright, (only five and a half years old) died the next day. Even in times of most profound grief, Jim was beaten.

His stepfather beat Jim whenever he acted up. He ridiculed Jim for carrying the family name that nobody else in the family shared with him, Ruzicka. (His siblings did not carry this name since his mother had remarried.) His own mother often did the same, telling Jim that he "was not welcome" or "did not belong" with the family.

On Jim's thirteenth birthday, his mother celebrated the day by taking Jim to the bus station, buying him a

ticket, and telling him, "Go be a man, live on your own."
His birth father had passed away before he was three years
old, and after years of being beaten and watching his
mother abuse alcohol and drugs, getting on a Greyhound
bus almost seemed like a reprieve, not a sentence. But the
abuse did not stop there.

Jim Ruzicka reluctantly explained, and it took years
to extract from him, that he had been sexually abused by
his uncle and sodomized repeatedly, which had confused
him. "Why would someone who is supposed to love me
and care for me do such things?" he asked. This was a
theme that played in his mind for almost two decades.
Jim's life was so abusive that he was constantly in fear of
what was to come next. He needed a place to escape to.

The woods behind the family home offered him
sanctuary. He would escape the beatings and sexual abuse
by disappearing for days on end into the dense woods
behind the Port Washington, Washington, family home. He

survived on what fish he could catch and by stealing from area homes when the occupants were at work. It was almost a given that people left their doors unlocked in rural Washington. There was no reason to lock them. During his formative years of the 1950s and 1960s, it certainly would be far more common to encounter an unlocked window or door.

Ruzicka easily entered these homes, grabbed something to eat, even lay down for a few hours, and left without anyone knowing he had been there. The abuse was verbal, physical, sexual, and psychological, and it was pervasive. The more important aspect of the abuse was the repeated trauma that Ruzicka endured.

Repeat trauma is when someone suffers from trauma over and over again, to the point that they compartmentalize it safely within their mind. It is not that the trauma does not exist; the mind simply needs a safe place to store the negative memory so that it is not constantly in their thoughts and actions. Thinking about what was to come each day would cause anxiety and fear. It was easier to simply accept the beatings as eventual rather than to presume they would go away.

The second trait of Jim Ruzicka, as it relates to the *Quadrant Theory of Violence,* is neglect. Neglect can take shape in many forms with children and teenagers. In Ruzicka's case, he was neglected by his mother and slighted by his birth father from the day he was born in 1950. He was born into a large family that could not afford the next child. It was odd that even though the family was destitute, his mother was constantly having children.

In a period of twelve years, Myrtle (his mother) attempted to have no less than ten children. She used children to help fulfill some psychologically unmet need, most likely major depressive disorder in today's terminology. She lost nearly half of her children before they reached the age of six. This was strange.

Whether it was the constant doctor visits to figure out what was wrong or his disappearing for weeks on end into the woods, Jim rarely saw his mother. When he did, she yelled at him even though he was basically living alone. Jim was forced to grow up very fast, since neither his mother nor his stepfather wanted him around. He often walked, unattended, to a small farmhouse for education, even as a very young child. While possessing an average IQ, he struggled with his studies from an early age. When he asked for help with homework, there was no one there to help. When he looked for help from friends or family, nobody was there. Jim admittedly had no friends.

When he needed basic school supplies, there were none. His mother used whatever funds she had to buy alcohol and drugs. When he needed food or water, he was told that he would only get breakfast that day or to go find water from another source besides the home. From his earliest memories, he recalled his mother and stepfather as being "neglectful." He was not provided with love, nurturing, tutoring, meals, proper nutrition, or counseling, nor was he given a home that was conducive to growing up peacefully. Like so many young children who grow up to become violent, the constant tumult of a violent parental relationship took its toll.

Ruzicka also explained that his parents argued constantly, and it often got physical. He watched as the arguments often escalated to hitting, slapping, throwing things at each other, or even greater violence. At times, his stepfather reared back and smashed his mother's face with his fist or whatever he could grab. It did not matter that young Jim Ruzicka was in the room. In fact, his stepfather relished in the fact that Jim saw the violence he was inflicting because this kept him in line.

One time, when he was around the age of ten, his stepfather was beating his mother so badly that Jim found a kitchen knife and stabbed him in the back. It was the first time that a knife felt like power. It was an instrument that brought about peace. It was personal, connected, and controllable. Knives became a big part of his life in their utility and their ability to protect his mother and himself from further violence. While he hated his mother for how she treated him, he explained, "She was still my mother, that was why I protected her."

The third trait found within the *Quadrant Theory of Predictive Violence* is abandonment. This trait is pervasive among almost all serial killers and was certainly present in the case of Jim Ruzicka. He was abandoned weekly by his mother as she pursued her next fix of drugs or alcohol. Jim stated that, "The weird thing was she would just disappear. A large, black car would come as I peered out the window. My mother would talk to the driver of the car then get into the back seat of the dark-colored vehicle. I do not recall exactly what type of car it was, but it almost looked like a Lincoln or Cadillac." When Jim asked his mother where she went, she would threaten to smack him in the face for questioning her. His stepfather did not even consider him part of the family.

Jim was so often abandoned that he had to fend for himself. He was regularly left with older brothers or sisters, aunts, uncles, or anyone who would look after him. Between his daily beatings from his stepfather, he returned to the woods for safety. He had his hiding spots, his "safe places," where nobody would find him. For Jim, it was better to be alone in the woods than be beaten. It was better to be alone than not be accepted by those who were supposed to love him. He was abandoned by teachers, who did not have time for his learning disabilities. He was often abandoned by friends, who made fun of how he dressed. Real friends were few and far between. His few friends often made fun of him for his glasses or "skinny body" shape. His "skinny body" was not by accident, it was because he was not given proper nutrition. Jim was even abandoned by school classmates because of his torn and tattered clothes, left alone to eat by himself. Bullied and shamed for what was not his fault, he regressed and began to resent those around him, particularly girls and women.

The final trait of the *Quadrant Theory of Predictive Violence* as it relates to violence is anger (self-hatred). When a child is abused, neglected, and abandoned, they often turn the blame inward toward themselves. The narrative becomes, *I cannot do anything right. Everyone hates me. I am no good. I want others to feel like I do. I want others to feel the pain I feel.* These are the exact words that Jim Ruzicka has repeatedly stated he said to himself. Over three decades with violent inmates I have heard the same or similar narrative in their minds as well. Over time, when some individuals are subjected to so much negativity and rejection, they want others to feel the same as they do. Their remorse becomes diminished at that time, because all they know is their own pain. While this is not intended to condone Jim Ruzicka's behavior in any way, it helps to provide a quick glimpse into how he was shaped as a child, as he reached puberty, and how he viewed the women he encountered later in life.

Jim Ruzicka despised his mother and all she stood for as a woman. He was rejected by girls at a young age for many of the reasons stated throughout this book and had difficulty with establishing normal intimacy. He was sexually abused, so he lacked the ability to choose his own sexuality since it had already been for him in some ways. While he will not go into the precise details of this sexual assault because it was so upsetting, he disclosed that the act changed who he was a person. At a time when Jim should have been forming his closest bonds, they were being shattered by the very people he was supposed to be able to trust.

This anger built up inside him, and he began to fantasize about revenge. Sexually, he was frustrated. He was not able to date women, and the few women who he was interested in ignored, abandoned, or rejected him outright. As the anger grew inside, Ruzicka began to take sex by force, committing at least two rapes and being convicted of one.

Jim Ruzicka was legally adjudged a "sexual psychopath," and was sentenced to serve ten years at Western State Hospital in Washington, but this would never come to pass. The rehabilitation would never occur because Ruzicka escaped after just nine months of sex-offender treatment.

The idea behind the hospital was to allow sex offenders to slowly assimilate back into society. Ruzicka was granted a furlough and scheduled to return to Western State Hospital on January 31, 1974. He would not return.

On that day, he called to check what time his group was to meet. After realizing they would be looking for him within a few hours if he did not show up, he decided never to return. He went to stay with his ex-wife, who lived not far from the hospital. Within two months of his escape, two young women were raped and murdered not far from their homes in Seattle, Washington.

A Modern Serial Killer Explained

Some criminologists might not consider Jim Ruzicka a serial killer by definition, although the modern definition has changed. A serial killer is someone who knowingly takes the life of two or more people, (not three or more) with a latent period ("cooling off" time) between each murder. Using the more modern approach to the definition, Jim Ruzicka is a serial killer.

In my professional opinion, not only would Ruzicka have gone on to kill dozens of girls, but his nomadic lifestyle would have made it far more difficult to link the crimes. His ability to travel from city to city within days, even hours, would have made him extremely dangerous.

Inmate Profile

Height: 6'1"

Weight: 153

Hair: Brown

Eyes: Brown

DOB: March 24, 1950

Marital Status: Divorced

Children: Daughter (not biological)

Years incarcerated: 48

Correctional Facility: Monroe Correctional

Institution

Inmate Number: 624728

Location of Crimes: Seattle, Washington

Convictions: Two Murders

Known Victimology: 15 to 21-year-old females

Prior Crimes: Attempted Rape While Armed with a

Deadly Weapon, Second Degree Assault,

Burglary, Attempted Burglary, Statutory
Rape, Rape

Additional Count of Rape (Ruzicka admitted to
only one rape at trial)

Prior Guilty Pleas/Convictions: Various sexual
assaults as a minor, ten-year suspended
sentence, adjudged a "sexual psychopath,"
and sentenced to serve time at Western State
Hospital

Motives for Murder: Anger, Self-Hatred, Revenge,
Sexual Gratification

Signature: Torture, Spending Time with Victims
(before, during, after the crimes)

Author Disclosures

Years of Communication with inmate: 5.5 (2017–Present)

Types of Communication: Written correspondence, phone calls, emails, pictures (inmate to author, author to inmate), personal artifacts from inmate

Provided money to inmate for physical stamps (to mail letters), electronic stamps (to send emails), artwork supplies, return shipping of artwork, quarterly packages, spendable account funds (when appropriate).

Inmate is destitute and, due to age and health, Jim Ruzicka cannot work. For these reasons, the above was not only needed but necessary to facilitate communication and shipment. This is commonplace for incarcerated individuals, particularly serial killers who receive heightened scrutiny inside

correctional institutions.

Forensic and Clinical Concerns

Confirmation Bias, Self-Disclosure, Malingering

Psychological Processes Utilized

Empathy, humility, and respect

Psychological Core Components

Autonomy, fidelity, veracity, self-respect,

beneficence

The following questions were submitted to Jim Ruzicka in July 2022. Jim Ruzicka's answers were signed and dated August 2, 2022.

1. When were you born?

   I was born on March 24, 1950.

2. Who were your biological mother and biological father?

   Myrtle Amelia Grinnell (mother. This was her maiden name, she was married) several times. Stanley Edward Ruzicka (May 10, 1921 – November 11, 1972) was my real father. I heard he died in California. My mother has died since I have been locked up.

3. How many brothers and sisters do you have, and what are each of their names, ages, and birthdays, that you can recall?

   I have three half-brothers and one half-sister (Myrtle Wright, Paul Wright, Wayne Wright, and

Morris Wright). I do not know their birthdays or ages from memory.

4. In doing familial research and requesting copies of several death certificates from the state of Washington, I found that many of your siblings died mysterious deaths. Can you confirm if my research on your siblings is correct?

Research:

Christine Louise Wright – Died at seven days old from an intestinal obstruction or pancreatitis on October 27, 1956.

John Ruzicka – Died five and a half months after his premature birth on May 16, 1948. The death certificate states, "cause of death unknown."

Linda Marie Wright – Died at five years old from congenital heart failure on July 25, 1957.

Edward Stanley Ruzicka, Jr. – Died at fifteen days old from an undisclosed cause on March 17, 1949.

Basil Arthur Wright – Born on September 4, 1953. Died five months later on January 22, 1954. The autopsy states that the cause of death was, "choking on milk curd."

Wayne Allen Wright – Death unknown (requested death certificate never arrived)

Ruzicka's response:

I cannot confirm the exact dates that you list, but I trust in your research. Linda died after heart surgery in Port Angeles, Washington, and the same for Morris I heard. The others I have heard about through hearsay only, since many were before my birth or before I was able to understand the nature of their deaths.

Death Certificate of Linda Wright, Jim's sister

This death was the most upsetting to Ruzicka, as he was present at the hospital when she died. He remembers screaming and even going on the outside ledge of the hospital room where his sister was being treated because no one allowed him to see her. This was among the most traumatic events early on in his life (occurred when he was seven years of age), and he continues to remark (six decades later) how deeply troubling it was to lose his younger sister. They were very close, and he remembers this event vividly.

Death Certificate of Stanley Edward Ruzicka, Jr., Jim's

brother

While Stanley did pass away shortly after his birth (fifteen days old), Jim Ruzicka was born almost one year to the day of Stanley's passing. He did not know that Stanley Jr. was born, much less died, until he was almost ten years old. The number of personal losses suffered by the family was almost unfathomable, with nearly half of the children dying before they reached the age of ten years old.

Death Certificate of Christine Wright, Jim's sister

This death occurred when Jim Ruzicka was six years of age. By the time Jim was seven years old, he had lost at least five siblings to premature, suspicious, or extremely rare medical conditions. According to further research, Basil died at five months of age from choking on milk curd. (His requested certified death certificate never arrived). How do you explain so many of your siblings dying from such odd causes?

> I have no idea, except my parents were always drinking and using drugs. I don't know if that had anything to do with their deaths.

5. Is it possible your mother, Myrtle Amelia Gilbert, and father, Stanley Edward Ruzicka, could have murdered any of their children?

> That is possible. I do not know the answer for sure. I know I was beaten a lot by them.

6. How did you process these deaths after learning about them?

I did not think of their deaths. I asked about the details of some of them, but never got an answer.

7. Is it true that you are the only remaining sibling with the last name of Ruzicka?

   Yes, as far as I know. I have a daughter who I gave my name when she was born. I was not her birth father.

8. Where did you attend grade school, and how do you think your schoolmates viewed your personality?

   I went to school in Port Angeles, Washington. I was always an outsider and stayed to myself most of the time.

9. Did you have many friends in grade school?

   No. I did not relate well to people.

10. Do you recall the name of your closest friend in grade school, and how long did you remain in contact with them?

    I never had any close friends in school.

11. Do you recall any favorite teacher's name or subject they taught?

I do not recall any of my teachers' names.

12. What was your fondest grade school memory?

My fondest grade school memory is of a girl who gave me a white German shepherd puppy. I never did learn the girl's name.

13. Did you like attending school in general?

I hated school since I had no friends, my fault, not theirs.

14. What is your most regrettable grade school memory?

Something that happened in Port Angeles, Washington. (Ruzicka did not elaborate further.)

15. Something disturbing happened to you on your thirteenth birthday. Can you explain this incident?

My mom says, "We are going downtown." I had the clothes on my back. She had a sack lunch peanut butter and jelly sandwich, a five-dollar bill, and a ticket to a Greyhound bus to go to Seattle, Washington. My mom said it was "time to grow up" and left me there. I was told to go visit my aunt and was abandoned by my parents. At that time, my mom and stepdad were into drugs really heavy.

16. How did you survive at thirteen years of age and where did you go?

I looked around and began to search for people who were in the same place I was, meeting a bunch of youngsters running the streets. Back then, nobody missed a kid abandoned by their parents. I literally grew up on the streets, stealing, mugging people and panhandling – whatever I and others like me could do to get money for food, dope, and booze is what we did. We would sleep any place we could find that was safe and out of sight. We couldn't go to the police as runaways, or they would lock us up.

If someone hurt one of us, the rest of us would go find that person and we would beat them down to hurt them back. We ran in what we called "packs," and often in groups of ten. We were like a family; from age thirteen to sixteen, survival was the name of the game. We did what we needed to do to survive. Whatever money we stole, we pooled at the end of the day so everyone could eat. You would see one of us, but all other the others were in sight of each other. Unless we wanted someone to know, they never knew all of us were there. They never knew we were there, as a group, in the hippie era, so we blended in with everyone else.

About 90 percent of the time when I hitchhiked or hopped a freight train, I had a variety of knives on me. I had one on my left forearm, one on my lower back belt, one in my right belt, one on my hip and one near my belt buckle – that was a novelty-type knife. I carried them for protection if needed, and felt safer with them.

I usually hopped freight cars and just ended up where they went to Portland, Oregon; San Diego, San Francisco, San Jose, Plano Beach, California; and even Boise, Idaho. There were many small towns along the way too. I would find an empty boxcar, but when the train stopped, I would get off and hide somewhere or I would find a car with big pipes on it, and crawl in one of them until they stopped. If we were caught, we would get beat up or worse in most cases. If I needed a longer rest period, I would find a hobo camp or hobo jungle, even then we always had to watch our backs. Hitchhikers have their own rules and codes. Some of the freight car tramps had their rules. No one really trusted each other, as we for the most part were loners. Being younger did not help.

I would get off whenever the urge hit me, to find a part-time job. I did not care where I ended up at most of the time. For longer trips, I carried a small canteen, a small amount of food, and, if I earned a few dollars working, I carried it in the heel of my boot or lining of my coat, wrapped in plastic.

I preferred hitchhiking. I did so in many cities, including at least five states. At the time, it was better to stay out of the South if you had long hair and no local ties.

I made it to a few places back east, but just there and gone. I was in Anchorage, Alaska, for a while, got in no trouble there. I got stabbed in the upper leg when a dude tried to rob me in Saint Louis, Missouri. I stitched my wound up with a needle and fine fishing line. I got the hell out of that part of the country. He got nothing from me except a sliced-up arm. I was lucky.

In most cases, I gave as much as I got. I carry a lot of scars from close calls. I overdosed on heroin and on speed once. Both were close calls.

Whenever I hopped a train, I seldom had any specific place I was going, just wanted to see the country, meet new people, and get lost. Most of the time, I never had any problems on the trains or when I got off somewhere.

Another way I would travel was to go to truck stops and volunteer to help load and unload whatever they were hauling. It saved them time from having to hire someone, and they also had company on long hauls. I headed to San Diego, California, from Seattle, Washington, and ended up in Redding, California, or San Jose, depending on the route we took. You could always ask one of the older tramps where specific trains were headed.

17. Where did you attend middle school?

In Port Angeles, Washington.

18. Did you have friends in middle school that you remember?

I had no real friends and never got close to anyone.

19. Do you recall a favorite middle school teacher or subject?

I do not know the teacher's name, but she taught an art class that I took.

20. Why do you think these teachers or subjects stand out as memories in middle school?

I liked art.

21. What is your best middle school memory?

My art class.

22. What is your least favorite middle school memory?

I always felt different and like an outsider.

23. How did your parents' divorce affect your opinion on abandonment and women?

I always thought all women were that way, and I got used to being alone. I would go into the mountain, hiking and camping alone, fishing and hunting alone. I never trusted women a lot.

24. What memories, if any, do you recall of childhood neglect?

I thought being abused and neglected was normal, as it was all I ever knew, so I ran away every chance I got.

25. I know this is a difficult question, but were you ever sexually abused?

Yes, two people were involved in the sexual abuse. A guy we called grandpa, and an uncle. They would force me so they could go "down on me." I was scared to tell anyone because if I told my mom, I would be called a liar and beaten. My stepdad beat me so many times from the ages of eight to eleven, but I had no one to turn to for help. I was scared I would get beaten worse than before if I told anyone about the sexual abuse, so it just continued.

My stepdad tried to do worse to me when he was drunk, so I hit him in the head and ran as fast as I could. No one could find me for over a week. I went to a creek I knew in the valley and caught fish to eat. I took small amounts of food from local homes around the valley. To get the fishing gear I needed, I snuck into homes late at night when no one was there and took the gear and a sleeping bag. I was nine to ten years old at the time, but I already knew how to survive.

26. What was the deepest childhood secret you held, that you never divulged to your parents?

That I hated and despised all adults with a passion.

27. In what ways do you recall your parents being abusive to you in any way (psychologically or physically)?

In all categories, psychological, physical, and mental. I thought it was normal, I became stubborn, rebellious, and hateful, and it screwed up my thinking and actions.

28. How did you internalize or process your abuse?

I accepted it as normal and hated all adults.

29. Do you attribute more of the abuse to your mother or your father?

More to my mom and stepfather, Paul Wright.

30. Did you ever feel self-hatred (feelings of worthlessness) in your own mind due to the repeated abuse you suffered?

Yes, 100 percent. I felt useless and worthless in every way.

31. Did you harbor any anger toward men or women?

More so toward women, as most of the bad treatment came from women.

32. Was your first sexual experience a pleasant one or disappointing? (e.g., first kiss)

The first time I had sex with a woman was when I got married the first time. It was pleasant, but I did not feel like I really knew what I was doing, if it was right, or if it was wrong.

33. What age were you when you had your first intimate experience?

I was twenty or twenty-one.

34. If you could undo one childhood memory, what would it be?

Learning to become closer with others in a pleasant way and not in a negative way.

35. Do you ever recall resorting to violence when you were under the age of fifteen, for anything?

When I saw my stepdad, uncle, and a guy we called grandpa beating my mom when they were all drunk. I stabbed my stepdad in the shoulder so they would stop, which they did. She was my mom no matter what.

36. Do you subscribe to the idea that human beings are born violent, or do you feel that violence is a learned experience?

People are born innocent; we learn to become violent with abuse and the negativity we experience.

37. Was your family religious and, if so, what ideology did you follow?

My family wasn't religious, and neither was I.

38. Did the family ever attend any religious celebrations?

Never to my knowledge.

39. Did you have faith in God as a child or teenager?

No. I had no faith in God as a kid because I couldn't understand how he could let others treat me as they did.

40. Do you feel God is vengeful?

God says an eye for an eye, a tooth for a tooth, then in the other testament he says, "Vengeance shall be mine, so sayeth the Lord." To me he was contradicting himself, saying two opposite things.

41. Do you feel that if you ask for forgiveness, all sins are forgiven?

I do not know for sure that God is vengeful. I am unsure about forgiveness.

42. Have you ever repented to a priest or clergyman/woman for your sins?

No. Most seem to talk a lot and I have never trusted them.

43. Why do you think you harbored feelings of violence against women?

I think because of the abuse and torment I received from my mom. I grew to harbor violence against women, thinking and feeling they were all the same way.

44. Before the two murders, can you try to explain your sexual compulsion behind the two prior sexual assaults or rapes?

    I was striking back at all women due to the way I was treated and brought up. The acts were purely revenge and not sexually motivated.

45. Did the incidents of revenge or hate further the violence against either of your two murdered female victims?

    If they looked similar in any way, or acted, or said something that struck a chord in me, I acted out in violence.

46. Did you say anything to either of your murder victims, who were both under the age of eighteen?

    I just told them, "Do as I say or die." I was stoned on drugs and booze, which made me even angrier.

47. Why do you think you chose to brandish a knife to control your victims over any other weapon?

I collected knives as a type of hobby and always carried one or more on me at a time. It is a weapon that is quick to use and quiet.

48. Why do you think you acted out in this way, at the young age of twenty-three?

My anger at the world and other people continued to grow as time went by. The one time I tried to get help, I was told it was natural for me to think and act as I did at my age. Not being able to get the help I knew I needed pissed me off even more.

49. What was your sentence and where were you incarcerated for the two rapes that preceded the murders?

I received two life sentences, and was sent to Walla Walla Penitentiary. (Here, Ruzicka either avoided talking about his prior rape convictions of thirteen- and fourteen-year-old girls, or he simply misread the question.)

50. Have your ever truly examined your attraction to thirteen- to sixteen-year-old girls, many of which you harmed by sexual assault, rape, or ultimately murder?

I am honestly not sure why. I regret what I did and can never change what I did. Who I was then is not the person I am now.

51. If you were charged with rape prior to the murders, please specify your exact sentence?

I was guilty, but the courts convicted me only for the murders according to the H-and-S paperwork I received. (Ruzicka continues to avoid speaking about the prior rapes of young girls.)

52. Were there any other rape victims, besides the known females, where you were never charged?

No. I was charged and convicted for the ones I committed.

53. Why do you think the judge sentenced you to serve a ten-year suspended sentence at Western State Hospital, given the gravity of the sexual assault and rape crimes?

I was given a choice, the Western State Hospital or prison. I chose Western State Hospital.

54. Did you serve your entire ten-year sentence at Western State Hospital?

No. Back then no one kept track of us at Western State, as long as we showed up back to the unit after we did our jobs. I was like a trustee, but my treatment got shoved aside and they dealt with others who were there and seemed to forget about me at the time. After going to my case worker at Western State Hospital and asking for further help with my problems, she said she couldn't help me, so I ran and got a ride from two workers there who had no idea I had to report back that day. I escaped early in the morning, around breakfast time, knowing that I had several hours before I needed to report to my unit around lunchtime. I called Western State Hospital and was told that nothing would happen to me if I came back late, but I just never went back. I left Western State and went to Seattle and stayed with my ex-wife and her husband. Her husband was the best man when her and I got married, and he married her after our divorce.

55. Did anyone help to facilitate your escape from Western State Hospital?

A friend helped me, who I had known for some time. I worked in the kitchen as a trustee and saw him eating breakfast. I asked him for a ride into town (Seattle), which he agreed to do and gave me a ride with his girlfriend.

56. Once you escaped, where did you go?

I went to Oregon, California, Montana, and Idaho, traveling, and then stayed in Seattle with my ex-wife and her husband, Chuck. (*It is during this time that many women could have been sexually assaulted or raped by Ruzicka in any or all these states. Often, rapists and murderers continue what they were doing in earnest upon escaping. There are too many cases to name that evidence this fact. As for additional murders, or what may have been his first, he has steadfastly maintained that no other cold case murders exist.*)

57. Did you commit any other sex crimes in other states?

Yes. Two cases that have never been mentioned occurred in Oregon, which I did a time for before being brought back to Seattle. One was for statutory rape. She was underage, so they nailed me for it, the other one was an older lady, but the attorney explained that that case had been dropped. I was guilty on both accounts and sentenced for the one. We were both high and she was underage, which I did not know at the time. All that counted was that I did it and did my time. I don't know why the other case was dropped.

58. Can you explain why your relationship between your ex-wife (whom you married on June 20, 1971, and divorced on October 5, 1972) ended?

Our marriage ended because I caught her having sex with her counselor in the Welfare Office in West Seattle. Then I caught her again with Chuck, who I thought was a friend up until that time.

59. Did you feel rage and anger after finding out she had not only cheated on you twice, but was living and now married to your former best friend?

I felt anger at both of them. At one point Chuck disappeared for four days, telling no one where he was. When I pushed for an answer, he said he went to Canada. Within a few weeks after staying with them, I was high and drunk. The night I left the house, I left in anger.

60. How quickly after leaving the house did you abduct sixteen-year-old Nancy Kinghammer?

Immediately. I didn't plan anything. I walked out of the house angry and went to the store. We got to talking in the convenience store and started walking together. I saw that we were alone, so I told her that my brother needed help and she was going to help. I took her into the woods and raped her, but it wasn't preplanned. When she called me a bastard and retard, I saw red and exploded. When I realized what I did, I tried to hide her body and left. It was about a half mile from my ex-wife's house at the time (two blocks from Nancy's home).

Crime scene photo – Nancy Kinghammer

Crime scene photo – Nancy Kinghammer

Crime scene photo – Nancy Kinghammer

Crime scene photo (Dirt removed for identification)

Crime scene photo after Nancy Kinghammer's body had

been removed

Ruzicka disputes that he wrapped Nancy's body with a carpet but admits to using a shower curtain from his ex-wife's house. He denies knowing why he went back to the house to get the shower curtain after killing Nancy, but he felt the need to do so. He suggests that feelings of remorse were a distinct possibility. Given that it would have been almost a mile round trip and subjected Ruzicka to interjecting evidence from his home to the crime scene, this was a very unusual aspect of the first murder. If Jim Ruzicka simply had left the scene, no further evidence would have tied him to the crime, save the knife, which offered few clues due to the lengthy exposure to the elements (twenty-nine days).

Ruzicka admits to placing Nancy's body under a few logs, with leaves and other debris to cover her body. He suggested that this was more to protect him from looking at what he had done rather than to evade detection for his crime. Nancy's body was discovered by Explorer

Scouts during a search about a week after Penny's body was found. Ruzicka steadfastly denies acts of necrophilia, though reports suggest he visited her body after the murder to engage in further sexual assaults.

Evidence, including a partial fingerprint found around Nancy's body on a shower curtain, led them to search for Ruzicka, who lived less than a half mile from this scene. After a door-to-door search of the area, they eventually were tipped off about Ruzicka's ex-wife living near the scene of the crime. Police confirmed that a knife left at the scene of this crime was similar in nature to several items owned by his ex-wife. His ex-wife also admitted that she was missing a shower curtain and believed her ex-husband (Jim Ruzicka) was seen leaving the home with it late at night.

Ruzicka explains that he did not use a knife on any of his victims, even if the knife was found at the scene of the crime. It is true, neither victim was stabbed, however torture marks were found and Penny's jacket was ripped on the outside, suggesting that he may have used the knife to scare her during the nearly hour-long time with him before she was murdered. Ruzicka denies torturing his victims, although much of the evidence and his own words suggest otherwise.

61. Explain why you chose Nancy Pauline Kinghammer?

It was happenstance, it was not pre-planned.

62. Nancy Pauline Kinghammer's body was found in a vacant wooded lot on February 15, 1974, in Seattle, Washington (King County). Had you ever been to this area before?

No, I had never been to this area before.

63. If you had never been to this area, never committed murder before, how did you know it would be secluded long enough to complete this act?

It was a large, wooded area and we were out of sight and hearing of anyone around. It was very late at night, too, around 11:00 p.m. to 1:30 a.m. (I do not really remember the exact time given my state of mind), so there were not many people around.

64. How much time did you spend with Nancy before she was murdered?

I spent a couple of hours with her. I was high and had been drinking and told her not to piss me off. We even smoked some weed and hash, mixed Together. (This is a revelation in more than twenty-five years of writing and speaking to serial killers and murderers. If Ruzicka is truly being honest, that the abduction occurred around 11:00 p.m. and she was murdered almost two hours later. It shows an unusual relationship with the victim.)

Many serial killers view their victims as mere objects, a means to fill a psychologically unmet need. Here, Jim Ruzicka states that although he took her into the woods under false pretenses and threatened her, he did not actually kill her for a few hours. This would be highly unusual behavior, for a perpetrator to befriend his victim, and then take her life nearly two hours later. It is far more likely this time was used to abuse, berate, or torture his victim.

65. Did you threaten her with a knife to keep her compliant and quiet?

    No, Nancy never saw or knew I had a knife. I threatened her verbally only.

66. Do you recall if Nancy said or did anything to remind you of your ex-wife?

    Yes, like my ex-wife, she was trying to act like she was better than me. True or not, I took offense to it until my anger built and I blew up in rage.

67. Do you think there was a catalyst, trigger, or act that angered you in such a way that you acted out violently?

    Yes, in what she said and how she said it, it made me boil inside. Eventually I lost control of myself.

68. Nancy Pauline Kinghammer's body was found in advanced post-mortem decomposition. However, even given this fact, her death was ruled consistent

with strangulation. Can you explain the details of how Nancy was killed?

I was on hard booze and mescaline at the time. I think the drugs played a part in the crime. Something told me to make her pay. I wanted to show her who was in charge. The physical looks of her drove me to talk to her. We talked for about fifteen minutes. We ended up off the side of the road. My intent was to do it enough (strangle her) to knock her out. I figured that would happen in this case, but she ended up dying. I kind of went crazy. I had remorse for what I did, which is why I covered up her body with debris at the scene. I did not bring a carpet or curtain or anything from my ex-wife's home. That is false. (This statement is untrue, as Ruzicka did bring items from his ex-wife's home.)

69. Since you lived very close to both victims, did you ever think about attending either of their funerals?

No. I did not. I did not know either victim personally.

70. Penny Marie Haddenham was only fifteen years old was she was abducted and killed on or around February 22, 1974, close to her home. Please explain how and why you chose her?

I did not plan to do it at first. We just talked and walked a bit. It had to do with her actions and speech. There was no reason at the time.

71. What time do you recall leaving your ex-wife's house? Specifically, what time do you think Penny's adduction took place?

I left my home around 10:00 p.m. I lived fifteen minutes away from where the crime was located. I know that I got back to my ex-wife's home right after 11:00 p.m. That is how I arrived at the idea that I spent about an hour with her in the woods.

72. How were you able to subdue Penny so quickly given she could have screamed, being so close to home?

I told her I would killer her and her family if she hollered, screamed, or tried to get anyone's help. The verbal threat was all it was at the time.

73. You stated many times in our conversations that you did not burn Penny or torture her before her death. How do you explain the reports of cigarette burns and bite marks on her body?

I never bit Penny nor burned her. If she was bitten or burned, it was by someone else. I raped and strangled her, yes. I never bit or burned or abused a woman besides taking her by force. I will even take a lie detector or truth serum test to prove every word I am saying herein is 100 percent true and accurate.

74. Did you hang Penny Haddenham?

I tied her to a tree root below the tree and against the dirt bank. How she got any other marks on her body, if there was such, was never done by me.

75. Did you take anything from her pockets after she was deceased?

Yes, I took about $8 that she had in her pocket. That was allegedly the money left over from the dress material she had bought.

76. Please explain the abduction of Penny Marie Haddenham, to the time you left the scene, with as much detail as possible?

Ruzicka stated he had gone over the exact details on a recorded call (transcribed later) and referred to this call for his answer to this question.

Crime scene photo – Penny Haddenham

There is some debate as to some of the forensics found at this crime scene. One of the two eyewitnesses who found Penny's body stated that he had witnessed police removing her clothes prior to the coroner arriving. Additionally, bite marks and burn marks were allegedly present on Penny's body, but Ruzicka denies any knowledge of inflicting these wounds. He has steadfastly denied torturing Penny for nearly six years and explains that this could not have been of his doing. That said, Ruzicka was a smoker and although he had never done this in the past, his crimes had escalated quickly in less than a month. Given the number of drugs he alleges he had in his system, the forty-eight years that have passed since the crimes or merely wanting to detail this information for a variety of reasons, he may never admit to torturing his victims.

Some of what Ruzicka admits is countered by the forensics. Semen was found under Penny's clothes, suggesting that not only was she sexually assaulted, Ruzicka had forced her to get dressed after the assault (Ruzicka may have also redressed Penny), then hanged her from the trunk of a tree. Ruzicka had just escaped from

Western State after being deemed a "sexual psychopath" by the judge. Ruzicka tends to be very forgetful on the numerous sexual assaults and rapes he committed throughout his life.

This has been the case for the better part of our relationship, when extracting information about these two murders. In one newspaper article from 1974, it suggests that Ruzicka abducted both girls from their homes, but this is patently untrue. Neither girl was abducted from their home. However, both encountered Ruzicka within a week of one another and both were murdered needlessly. If Ruzicka were truly under the influence of mescaline, alcohol, or other drugs, he likely would not have been able to control either girl or perform sexually. Given his lifelong poor vision (which was even worse at night), it would have been very hard for him to see while in wooded areas, yet he denies the obvious. Jim Ruzicka knowingly, forcibly, and willingly abducted, raped, and murdered two girls within a

week in February 1974.

Crime scene photo – Penny Haddenham

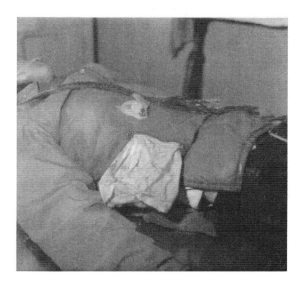

Crime scene photo – Penny Haddenham

77. Did you feel any remorse for Penny's death afterward?

At the time, no, I tried to forget what I did. Years later I wished I could have had remorse.

78. Did you ever think about attending Penny's funeral as a means of making amends?

No, I did not. I did know either of the victims.

79. According to Vital Statistics as well as their corresponding death certificates, it appears that Nancy was killed first, but Penny's body was found first. Is this correct, to your knowledge?

I am honestly not sure who was found first. I heard it was Penny, but I never knew beyond hearsay.

80. Is there anything you want to clarify regarding either of these two abductions and murders?

At no time was a knife used, neither victim was bitten, abused, or burned by me. All of that information is false.

81. How long was your criminal trial?

It was about a month. Maybe a couple weeks.

82. What do you recall as being the most incriminating evidence against you at trial?

The fact that I was living in the area at the time, partial fingerprints, and a shower curtain. They tied the shower curtain to my ex-wife's place because I had been in trouble in Port Washington all my life.

83. How did the police connect a shower curtain (used to wrap Nancy Kinghammer's body) to you?

Supposedly, they went around asking people in the neighborhood near where the two bodies were found. They questioned everyone if they were missing a shower curtain, and my ex-wife said that hers had been taken. She said the last time she had seen it, it was in my possession. I do not know what else she said to the police, but it was enough for them to connect me to the crime.

84. You have been incarcerated for forty-eight years. If you could redo your whole life, what age do you think you would begin?

If I could redo my whole life, I would choose to do so as a kid. To grow up in a decent home, around decent people, and with loving parents to help me as most parents do.

85. If you had a time machine, what age would you travel back to and why?

I would travel back to the time of Nancy and Penny's deaths, to prevent what I did and prevent their deaths. They did not deserve what I did to them. I was totally screwed up in every way, always high and on booze.

86. If there was a single moment, one trigger, what do you think it was that forever changed the trajectory of so many lives?

The one moment was really many. Growing up, the abuse, physical and mental, that screwed up my thinking and actions. It took years to learn that and to change. It is not that changing or becoming better means anything to anyone but me.

87. What is one thing about yourself that you have changed since your incarceration?

Since my incarceration, my attitude and outlook of women has changed. The way I think and act and that I continue to strive to better myself as a person. I hate who and what I was prior to being locked up.

88. Do you think men and women can do the same job and be considered as equals?

Yes. I believe men and women can do the same and even different jobs and be considered as equals.

89. Where would you be today if you were not where you are right now?

If I were not here, I would be in the country someplace, living a decent and peaceful life.

90. You have repeatedly stated to me that you do not present a risk, that you would be a reformed inmate and, if paroled, you would present a low risk of re-offending. Given the gravity of your crimes, how can you assure the public this is true?

I have learned how screwed up I was growing up, and hatred is no longer a part of my life. Drugs and booze are no longer a part of my life, and I strive to better my life every day. I know that no one cares that I am in prison, and I know I will die here. No one is interested in me getting out and giving me a chance to prove I have changed. I am to blame, no one but myself, for doing what I did and being in here. I feel remorse for what I did, more than words alone can ever begin to express.

91. Is it true that you died in prison (from COVID-19) in 2021 for several minutes and were revived? Can you explain what happened?

Yes, from what I was told, I died twice. All I saw was blackness, total blackness and quiet. It was not bad; it was like a black board, a chance to start over with a clean slate or my future. It was one of being alone and traveling either to heaven or to hell, and not knowing which one to choose, from what I have been told.

92. Do you think God has forgiven you for your actions (if you believe in a God or a higher power)?

I believe God has helped me learn and grow to change for the better as a person. As far as forgiveness, I do not think anyone can or will forgive me for my past and all the things I have done. I will not know if God has the will until the day of reckoning comes.

93. What is one stress habit that you continue to exhibit?

   When I am stressed, I withdraw into a shell of my own making.

94. What is a stress habit that you have eliminated from your life?

   One stress habit that I have eliminated is thinking about my past. I have learned that no one is to blame for my past, thoughts, feelings, and so on, except me, myself. No matter how I was treated, abused, and so on, I chose my own path, being crazy, being bad, I chose it. As a kid, that was the easy way out, to blame others. I have learned the opposite as the years have gone by.

95. Do you use anything to sleep with at night to bring you comfort?

   I toss and turn most nights. In prison, one rarely finds comfort of any kind. I am paying for what I did and that is a type of comfort, knowing that no matter what, even if I was out, that I would never do anything wrong again.

96. Do you think about 1974 often or would you rather move on, knowing you have done all you can at this point?

Until my death I will think about 1974 and what I did. And I will continue to repent what I did every single day and every single night.

97. Do the faces of Nancy Kinghammer and Penny Haddenham ever haunt you in your sleep?

Yes, both have haunted me because they did not deserve what I did or to die. But I regret what I did with all my heart, body, and soul and always will.

98. Would you consider yourself an introvert or an extrovert?

I am more of an introvert, shy and withdrawn, but I get along with others now, whereas in the past I did not.

99. If you were to be released, given your age, limited education, and ongoing health issues, how would you care for yourself?

I would like to work, so I would get any job that would hire me and work my way from there. I have a lot of job skills. I rely on my abilities to work and, if needed, to start to get housing help and medical help until I could get on my feet. I have a high school diploma and need only five credits of algebra to get my associates degree. I would like to get that even it means taking a night or home course to do so.

100.   What level of risk to you think you still pose to the public?

I am no longer a threat to society or anyone else, through learning on my own and counseling. I have learned to change, learned why I did what I did, and why I acted as I did. I have learned to talk to others if and when I need help. I would take classes for drug and alcohol (Alcoholics Anonymous) and NA (Narcotics Anonymous) classes. I would also go to counseling weekly. Plus, my age and health. I am no longer a threat and I do not wish to ever hurt or abuse anyone ever again and would stop anyone I seen doing so.

101.   Please provide any final words, clarifications, or thoughts wherein these questions may have missed, were mistaken in date, time, person, place, or context?

Ann Rule wrote some things about me that were 100 percent false. She said I was into bestiality, which I never was, nor accused of, never arrested, or convicted of, and I placed more value on animals than humans at one point. Animals are loyal and loving, and I always treated animals with the highest respect.

I beat a guy up as a teenager because he threw some puppies in a river in a gunny sack off a bridge. Ms. Rule also said things about my family that were never true. She put what she thought would make things more sensational.

I am no longer filled with rage, as I was when I was younger. I have learned to deal with the psychological, physical, and mental abuse I went through growing up as a child. I have learned to open up and left others in. I know, realistically, that society is going to judge me on what I say or do. They are not going to let me out to prove I have changed and can be a useful member of society and I accept that I will die in prison. I do not hate anyone for that or for thinking what they do.

Regardless of what I went through growing up, I

was stupid, and let drugs and booze control my life.

Prison will turn you into an animal, or you can

change for the better. I chose to grow and change

for the better in every way as a person, not because

I was forced to do so but because I hated who I was

and wanted to better myself as a person, which I

have done and will continue to do, no matter what.

—Jim Ruzicka

03-24-50

Official Death Certificate of Nancy Pauline Kinghammer

The state of Washington allows non-family to request death certificates. These certificates were vital in establishing the information contained within this book to corroborate dates, cause of death, birth dates, and other important data. It confirms that, at least according to the data, Nancy was murdered first, with Penny's body being found first.

Official Death Certificate of Penny Marie Haddenham

The certificate and cause of death dispute Jim Ruzicka's claims that he did not hang Penny Haddenham. There was nothing to suggest anyone else was involved, and when police arrived, she was hanging by the same rope as Ruzicka described. Ruzicka admits that he tied the rope around a stump of the tree, but his explanation becomes murky when compared to the crime scene photograph. It appears, from all the available evidence, that Penny was redressed after being sexually assaulted, then hanged.

Age Inconsistencies on Death Certificates

In numerous books, online articles and podcasts that incorrectly list Penny Haddenham's date of death at fourteen years of age. This is completely untrue. The certified death certificates (Provided by the Washington Office of Public Health), prove that she died at the age of fifteen. Additionally, Nancy Kinghammer is often listed on the internet, numerous publications, and podcasts as being killed at the age of fifteen, which again is erroneous information. Nancy died at the age of sixteen. These inconsistencies, along with which body was found first, have surfaced in similar ways and wrongly so.

From the advanced state of decomposition of Nancy's body, coupled with these two documents, we know that Nancy was the first to be abducted but the second to be found by searchers. Penny's body was found by happenstance, whereas Nancy's body required a more exploratory search. Explorer Scouts along with local police would eventually find Nancy's body.

Using the last known dates both were alive, given what is known about how quickly Ruzicka murdered each victim, makes for a clearer picture of what actually happened. Sadly, it may have been a simple disagreement over a television show with her sister that led Nancy Kinghammer to leave her house. Irritated enough to leave, she encountered Ruzicka by pure happenstance on February 15, 1974, and was killed that very same day. Penny Haddenham, in a similar way, was searching for dress fabric, stopped off at a friend's house around 8:30 p.m. on February 21, 1974, which was the last time she was ever seen alive. Penny encountered Jim Ruzicka on February 21, 1974. She was abducted, raped, and killed that very same evening.

Penny's body was discovered in the woods by a newspaper boy on March 12, 1974, nineteen days after being abducted. Only after Penny's body was discovered, figuring both girls were likely killed by the same killer, was a search ordered of all wooded areas. The search took place, and Nancy's body would be found by Explorer Scouts on March 16, 1974, twenty-nine days after her murder.

Had it not been for both girls being in the wrong place at the wrong time, when Jim Ruzicka's rage was boiling over, both would likely be alive today. They would have enjoyed life, attended college, graduated, gotten married, and had their respective families and friends, living what most of us expect as commonplace lives. Instead, they met a revenge-filled, sexually sadistic man who was hell bent on revenge and looking to "make someone pay" for all the wrongs in his life.

Phone Interviews Regarding the Last Moment of Each Victim's Life – As told by Jim Ruzicka

I have fielded more than 200 phone calls from Jim Ruzicka since 2017. Phone calls often occur at the rate of two to three times a week. I have utilized this format of communication because it is easier to detect emotion, malingering, hesitation, pauses of thought, and a variety of other things that no other reliable medium offers. While I remain on Ruzicka's visitation list, you are not allowed to write down or record any information, which makes that method not only impossible but transcribing his answers in verbatim form would be impossible. So, as with many other inmates that I have interviewed in both private and public, the telephone was utilized to get this information. Much of it was not easy for Ruzicka, as he knows calls are recorded. In many ways, it is far easier to respond in writing, which is why that medium was used for the other questions. It also opened the avenue to speak about it verbally.

A note on the difficulty of telephone interviews. This is a verbatim transcript of a phone call surrounding the method of operation, abduction, and murders of Penny Marie Haddenham and Nancy Kinghammer. This call was recorded, with Ruzicka's permission, on September 7, 2020, at 11:46 a.m. EST. The call lasted twenty minutes and forty-six seconds.

Due to the impersonal nature of gathering such traumatic information from the inmate (Jim Ruzicka does not like to recall the details of these two murders), it was best to utilize this form of communication. Additionally, getting specificity to his answers and listening to how the questions were answered, noting any unusual emotions, volume changes, pauses, or possible malingering, was best completed using a telephone.

The Murder of Nancy Kinghammer

Jim Ruzicka's first victim – Nancy's body was located after the second victim's body was found.

Anthony Meoli: "With Penny you admitted to taking four hits of LSD before killing her. Was it the same with Nancy?

Jim Ruzicka: "I was on mescaline then and some hard booze."

Meoli: "Do you think the drugs were taken to diminish what was going to happen?"

Ruzicka: "Yeah, that was part of it, took away from my inhibitions, took away from being scared. After the second one happened, I took off by myself to be alone."

Meoli: "Can you walk me through how you encountered Nancy Kinghammer?"

Ruzicka: "Her and one of her friends were walking together. I guess it was a friend. They stopped, and one of them went into her house. She came out, started walking, took off alone. She turned around near where she lived, and then I saw her. Something inside of me just said, 'make her pay.' I grabbed her by the arm and took her back into the woods."

Meoli: "'Make her pay?' Was that the same theme that ran through your mind before you abducted her?"

Ruzicka: "No, this had to do with the way a couple of my aunts treated me, so I wanted to get back at them. I wanted to tell her (Nancy), 'Hey you're not in charge, I am.'"

Meoli: "Nancy was only sixteen at the time, what do you think made you think of how your aunts treated you?"

Ruzicka: "Her looks, her physical looks, they could have been spitting images of each other."

Meoli: "Was there any conversation between you and Nancy prior to her abduction?"

Ruzicka: "Uh, just regular chit chat."

Meoli: "How long did you talk?"

Ruzicka: "About fifteen minutes."

Meoli: "Then what happened?"

Ruzicka: "We ended up off the side of the road."

Meoli: "Did you see an opportunity with her to enact violence?"

Ruzicka: "Yeah, unfortunately yes."

Meoli: "So you took the opportunity?"

Ruzicka: "Yes. I strangled her once we were in the woods."

Meoli: "Was she sexually assaulted?"

Ruzicka: "Yes."

Meoli: "Unlike Penny's body, which was openly

displayed after her murder, you did the

opposite in this case, is that correct?"

Ruzicka: "Yes. I was trying to do something; I was

ashamed of what I just did. I was just trying

to put it out of sight, not so much for others,

but to hide it from myself, so I didn't have to

look at it." (Nancy's body was covered with

leaves and debris.)

Meoli: "Did you use anything to cover up Nancy's

body?"

Ruzicka: "No, they said that there was a drape from

my ex-wife's house, right. I couldn't figure

that one out. I didn't take any drapes from

my ex-wife's house. So, how a drape ended

up there, I have no clue. I did not get one."

(This was an odd response given that Jim

Ruzicka readily admitted to taking a shower

curtain after the murder and coming back to the crime scene to cover up the body. How Jim, forty-eight years later, could not see a correlation between the word drape and a shower curtain remains unclear, even when asked.)

Meoli: "Was she wrapped in any way?"

Ruzicka: "No." (Again, this is incorrect information, as she had been wrapped in a shower curtain taken from his ex-wife's house. This was among several clues left at the scene that eventually tied Ruzicka to the murders.)

Meoli: "She was naked?"

Ruzicka: "Yeah. But everything was laying over top of her."

Meoli: "Did you stab her or just show her your knife?"

Ruzicka: "I just showed them each my knife. I never stabbed anybody, none of my victims. I didn't cut them or stab them with a knife."

Meoli: "So the knife was used just to strike fear in them?"

Ruzicka: "Yeah."

Meoli: "Why do you think since you had a knife on you that you chose such an intimate form of murder as strangulation?"

Ruzicka: "I don't know. I honestly don't know. I have had other people ask me that same question over the years and I still haven't been able to figure that one out."

Meoli: "Do you think that a knife would have been too messy for you?"

Ruzicka: "Probably. It was not so much about being easier. My original intent was to choke her just enough to just knock her out. I've had people choke me and I'd end up blacking

out when they were doing it. I figured that

this would happen in this case and then I

could just turn around, just get the hell out

of dodge."

Meoli: "Did you think you were just going to knock

her out?"

Ruzicka: "Yeah, that is what I thought at the time.

And when I realized what I had done, I kind

of went crazy."

Meoli: "So there was some remorse shown at the

crime scene by you covering up her body?"

Ruzicka: "Yes, yes, there was. Right now, today, if I

could give my life and bring back the two

lives that I took, I would. Most people

would say those are just words. To me they

are not, they are not just words, they are

fact. I would do that."

Meoli: "What do you think you would say to the victims now?"

Ruzicka: "I would tell them I am very sorry, and I would ask for their forgiveness."

Meoli: "I appreciate you talking to me about this difficult subject, I know it is not easy to talk about."

Ruzicka: "No problem, thank you."

The Murder of Penny Haddenham

Anthony Meoli: "So getting back with Penny, you meet her, you talk to her for a good bit of time, do you walk together?"

Jim Ruzicka: "We walked for, what, about one, two, probably three-and-a-half blocks and we came to another cross street. I was looking around, there was nobody around us or anything else, and I saw the woods. And I turned around and said, 'Well, we are going to go for a walk.' I took her arm and told her, 'Don't raise any hell or make any noise.' And I had a knife at the time, and I showed her the knife. Then I put it back and put it away. At that point, I hadn't planned on doing anything. When it happened, originally, I just wanted somebody around that I could sit and talk to, and we talked for a good forty to forty-five minutes, even when we were in the woods, before anything happened."

Meoli: "So you are in the woods, but it is late at night, correct, so it's pretty dark?"

Ruzicka: "Yeah, it was about 1:30 a.m. in the morning, plus being in the woods like that, it was a little darker. All you had was the moonlight."

Meoli: "So you took her into the woods with her, all alone, but you forcibly took her back there, did she think that something bad was going to happen to her?"

Ruzicka: "She didn't say. She did not say if she was scared. She didn't seem scared. I had put the knife away, I put it back up, and the way I was holding her arm, I let go of it and we

just hold on to her hand … and walked like
normal."

Meoli: "Was she bound in any way so that she
could not leave?"

Ruzicka: "No. She could have run away. I think she
trusted me."

Meoli: "How far apart we you?"

Ruzicka: "Uh, about two feet."

Meoli: "So this was a very close contact
conversation?"

Ruzicka: "Yeah."

Meoli: "Why do you think she didn't run, even
though you had brandished a knife taking
her back there?"

Ruzicka: "She made no attempt to leave whatsoever."

Meoli: "So what happened next, what was the thing
that you can remember?"

Ruzicka: "She compared me to one of her boyfriends,
            I guess it was a boyfriend, one of the guys
            she knew – and she turned around and said,
            'You are starting to act like him, being an
            asshole.' When that was said, just went
            lights out, took a different turn."

Meoli: "Did the anger that had boiled up inside you,
            that brought you to take her into the woods,
            suddenly turn ten-fold worse?"

Ruzicka: "Yup."

Meoli;   "Why do you think you sexually assaulted
            Penny Haddenham?"

Ruzicka: "Uh, I don't know. Just an afterthought, is
            the only way I can explain it."

Meoli: "Was she sexually assaulted or raped after
            she was killed?"

Ruzicka: "No. Nope, she was not." (There was some
            hesitation when answering this question. I

detected some malingering when answering this question. Whether it was the gravity of the question or because this was a very uncomfortable topic—necrophilia – which many serial killers have denied when evidence suggested otherwise, such as, Ted Bundy—there was a noticeable pause here.)

Meoli: "How long did the sexual assault last do you think?"

Ruzicka: "Probably about twenty minutes."

Meoli: "At the time when the act was completed (rape/sexual assault), did she think she was going to be okay?"

Ruzicka: "Yeah, as far as she knew. What made me so angry and blew a fuse was there was a length of the rope on the ground. I don't know where it was from or what it was from, but she had it, she picked it up, and, when she did, she turned around and slapped me across the face with it and called me an asshole. That is when I seen red."

Meoli: "Did you use your hands around her neck (to strangle her)?"

Ruzicka: "No, I took the rope and used it."

Meoli: "Where did you get the rope from?

Ruzicka: "She picked it up off the ground, laying on the ground, right where we were. It looked like part of what used to be an old sling or something, because you could see a piece of rope hanging off the tree where somebody had tied it off."

Meoli: "So you used the piece of rope that she had found?"

Ruzicka: "Yeah. Yup. I used what she picked up off the ground. There was a bank, and a root came out and I tied it around the root."

Meoli: "Why do you think you did this?" (Hanging

            Penny with the rope)

Ruzicka: "I haven't got a clue. I don't really know. I

            really don't."

Meoli: "Did you stop at any time to look at what

            you had done, or did you leave the scene

            immediately?"

Ruzicka: "No, afterward, I looked around, and got

            scared. I knew what I did was wrong, and I

            didn't know what I could do to fix it."

Meoli: "What do you think the thoughts going

            through your head were at that time?"

Ruzicka: "All sorts. Get the hell out of dodge, don't

            let anybody see you, hide. The word 'run'

            kept going through my head."

Meoli: "Was there any comfort in that it was

            nighttime, so you could not see what you

            had done really well?"

Ruzicka: "Yeah, some. I did not want to dwell on the fact of what I did. I did everything I could to cover it up. When I finally did get back home, I went through a bottle and a half of Jack Daniels, smoked a whole bunch of weed, did some more acid, and a just a lot of everything else. The next morning, about 6:00 a.m., or 6:15 a.m., somewhere in there, I opened my dresser drawer, took my money out, took all my money, put my money in my pocket, grabbed a couple packs of smokes from the cupboard, and hit the road, went to California. I had money to buy a bus ticket, but I turned around and just went out to the freeway and started hitchhiking."

Meoli: "How were you caught after the crimes?"

Ruzicka: "I went to Oregon and committed statutory rape on a thirteen-year-old girl. I met this gal and her friend in downtown Portland. A kid was trying to talk to her and a friend to get them to try to leave with him. I knew the dude from the streets, his brother was a pimp and send his younger brother out to hustle other girls. Anyhow, I let them know what was going on and they left him and asked me to ride the bus with them to Beaverton, Oregon."

"When we got there, the other gal left, leaving me alone with the younger one. I was walking her home. I asked her if she smoked weed and she said, 'Yes.' So we smoked some Columbian weed. We ended up in an empty parking lot behind a small church. We got to making out and she ended up with nothing but her panties and me in my shorts. We smoked more weed and during that, I slid her panties and my shorts off. After a bit I got on top of her and started pushing myself in, that is when she said she was a virgin. At no time did she say, 'No.' After that she said, 'That the first time I did it with anyone, I am glad I did.' We also did it in a nearby field. They caught me that night."

"I did not know how old she was at the time, but she reported me to the police. When they picked me up, I gave the name, Troy Asin. (Meaning to commit a sin.) I had shared this nickname as a joke with another inmate who I got to know while I was at Western State Hospital named Carl Harp."

"Harp's name came up when police checked out both names, thinking it was an odd name to have in the database, not once but twice.

After finding out that my name was fake, along with my ex-wife talking to local police, they put two and two together. I was taken from Oregon to Seattle, Washington, for processing for the escape and eventually some evidence caught up to me, including a partial fingerprint at the scene of the crime and the shower curtain."

Meoli: "How long did your trial last?"

Ruzicka: "It lasted about three to four weeks, then the jury found me guilty on both counts of murder. My ex-wife helping the police did not help matters."

Meoli: "Do you have a final statement you would like to make?"

Ruzicka: "I blame only myself for being in prison regardless of how I was treated growing up. Yes, I robbed and stole to survive. In the end, I committed the crimes I did, then I

blamed everyone else. In reality, it was my

fault. I was trying to hurt others for the way

I had been hurt."

"I feel more remorse than words can ever

begin to express. I pray for my victims every

night and wish I could bring them back.

What I did will haunt me forever. No one

wants to get to know me for who I am now,

that I have changed. I do not blame them

because of what I did. I am not the same

person I used to be and never will be."

"Sometimes growing up we take on traits

and attributes that we learn, both from the

way we were treated and how we were

raised. That is not an excuse, I pray to the

good Lord that I will be forgiven with all my

heart. Whatever my fate may be, I accept

and blame only myself for who I used to be.

I am different now, but realize I know most

people in society do not care if I have

changed or not. I have learned to face life

and take responsibility for what I did and

how I used to be."

—Jim Ruzicka

Conclusion

I have amassed nearly six years of correspondence with Jim Ruzicka in almost every possible way. From video conferencing, handwritten letters, e-mails, and telephone calls to receiving personal items that were mailed by Jim. The personal items he created told me how he thought in his spare time, which added another level of knowledge.

Some of the items Ruzicka sent included beadwork, paintings, detailed drawings, leatherwork, sketches, and even his old, broken LED television. There is almost nothing that Ruzicka has not shared with me in some way at this point. As to the number of hours I have spoken to him, it numbers in the hundreds. As to the total number of handwritten letters (many more than ten pages in length), they number well over two hundred. The number of e-mails would exceed two hundred as well. Artwork, including sketches, paintings, and custom playing cards - numbers in the hundreds. As for personal visitation, the 2,800 miles and COVID-19 (both for domestic flights and prison quarantines) made this impractical. Additionally, no recording of any kind is allowed at the facility.

I have shared with you all I know about Jim Ruzicka in its rawest form. These were his words to crimes that shocked the state of Washington and stunned a nation in 1974. Ruzicka is far less known than other serial killers due to the number of victims, the time (1974), and his relatively quiet nature. He readily admits that he is sorry for what he did and would give up his life for the two victims just about every time he writes. In my professional and clinical opinion, I do believe he has remorse, but I also believe he has moved on from what he did for his own self-preservation.

It is a difficult world to live in when the deepest, darkest things you ever did are well known to the entire world. He has done his best to explain these abductions and murders. He struggled at times, even crying, recalling the nuances that led him down a very dark path in his life, taking the lives of two young women.

This was 1974, the nation was just about to celebrate its bicentennial, and things were relatively calm. I was a child growing up during this decade, and remember the decade for its lack of technology, simplicity, lack of excess, and limited access to things, including gasoline. We rode bikes alone, we traveled miles from home as children without much worry, no one locked doors, and often we ran errands for our parents or ourselves —as Penny was doing to get material for her dress—without ever thinking about what might happen to us.

Horror movies were just beginning to come out, but were not nearly as mainstream nor as violent as we see today. Looking back, the mid 1970's might have been the last time in America where we saw each other for what we were. We dressed in odd looking clothes, but in many ways we all dressed alike. Racial issues, while surely existing, were not on the forefront of newspapers, and we prepared as a nation to remember our freedom, together, as one. The American flag meant something to everyone, and burning it was blasphemy.

Jim Ruzicka shocked the state of Washington in less than two weeks' time. Within just a few weeks of his escape from Western State Hospital, he had murdered two innocent girls and destroyed their families forever.

The crime also affected many in the area instantly. After the first abduction, kids who once rode their bikes alone were now barred from doing this activity. Neighbors began locking their doors, fearing he may not be the only perpetrator. Seattle, Washington, and the two counties where these crimes took place, not far from one another, would never recover from these crimes. The 1970's would never be the same for anyone near these crimes, and their towns have never forgotten what Jim Ruzicka did. He took their innocence away.

Those who found both of the bodies were children. The boy who found Penny hanging from a tree was a newspaper boy. What he saw shocked him so much that he told his sister not to come down the heavily wooded path. Allegedly, he and his father rushed to a nearby home to call the police but were met with resistance. Eventually police were called, but the damage of seeing what Ruzicka did was done. The boy and his father would never forget that scene.

In the case of Nancy Kinghammer, horribly, the scene was not much different. While the police and locals were out searching for her, it would be Explorer Scouts who found the body. Without a doubt, the decomposition of her body and seeing what they saw that day will never leave their memories. For the police in King County, it would be two of the worst crimes any of them saw during their tenure as police officers. It affected everyone and everything forever. Jim Ruzicka ruined many lives by trying to make others feel as he felt.

As a clinician and someone who has invested so much time with Ruzicka in going over his involvement with sexual assault, rape, and murder, there can be some resulting lack of shock because I have lived these stories for the better part of a decade. I have gotten to know Ruzicka in ways that nobody has gotten to know him. I know that he would present a significant danger to the public if it were not for his advanced age and failing health. Sex offenders and rapists do not usually rehabilitate easily, if at all, and the knowledge that sex was little motivation for these crimes tells us that he presents a real danger.

Serial killers are as different as much as they are alike. As you have read with regard to my *Quadrant Theory of Predictive Violence* (abuse, neglect, abandonment, anger), it holds true in almost all of the serial killing cases I have studied.

In the present case, all four components were shown. Ruzicka's mental and physical abuse was early, often and severe. His neglect resulting in him seeking the woods behind the home to rely on scraps of food stolen from neighbors. His father would later reject him as a son – explaining that he was "not a Ruzicka" before he died. His mother and stepfather abandoned him in almost every instance where they should have parented their young child.

Jim Ruzicka harbored resentment toward his mother and all of the women who had rejected him. This anger and self-hatred were furthered when he discovered that his former best friend, and the best man at his wedding, was now living with his ex-wife. This was the final stressor for him. Jim Ruzicka, a man who had difficulty expressing appropriate feelings and sexuality, now had the opportunity to express his misplaced and unrepentant rage.

Where I disagree with the lack of a sexual component as a motive, particularly the prior rapes and even the sexual assaults of his two murdered victims, was his willingness to blame drugs and alcohol on each of these occasions. For many years I listened to Ruzicka's recollection of the crimes. Until the questionnaire and final phone interview, I had never heard about substance abuse as a repeated excuse for his actions. In each of the rapes, even the underage statutory rape case in Oregon, he blamed the fact that he was on drugs. Ruzicka, in this crucially important area of culpability, does not take responsibility for his actions.

Drugs and alcohol would not be an excuse, rather a comorbid reason for his actions. If we look to the nature of his crimes, they were seemingly unplanned in his descriptions, yet he had brought a knife to each of the scenes. We know this because he told us this was the case. Ruzicka minimizes bringing the knife by saying that he never stabbed his victims. While this does appear to forensically match the pathology reports, dismissing the presence of a scary knife to a young girl shows his lack for humanity. Forty-eight years later, it shows that Jim Ruzicka does not fully understand the graphic nature of his crimes.

Brandishing a weapon, in the middle of the night, to a teenager girl — both of which were much smaller in height, weight, and strength—shows its own level of misguided revenge. Ruzicka surely knew these young girls would quickly comply with his demands. In one case he says that all he did was use his voice, but the threat was very real. To say, "I will kill you and your family" would make almost anyone cower in fright. I do not believe that Jim Ruzicka only used his voice, I believe he brandished his knife, wrapped in black tape (shown on the rear cover of this book), and showed it during each victim. He wanted to scare these young girls into submission, fast, control the scene, and move them into a secure location, out of sight.

We know from his childhood that Ruzicka spent many days, weeks, and even months in the woods behind his home to escape the violence he saw and the abuse that his mother and stepfather enacted against him. Ruzicka was comfortable in the woods. He likely knew these areas to be safe, far enough away from the street, and likely did not simply happen upon either scene. Ruzicka was a career criminal insofar as sexual assault and rape. He had committed at least four to six sexual assaults before his incarceration at Western State Hospital. When he was released, he could have gone anywhere, but he chose to go to his ex-wife's home. There, he only found more of what he was looking for, an excuse to enact revenge while committing unwanted sexual acts and eventually murder.

It is my professional opinion that the motive behind both killings was revenge, but it did not end there. Ruzicka sexually assaulted both of his victims before and possibly even after the crimes (necrophilia). While there is no real way to prove necrophilia, some of this was conjecture based upon anecdotal information from police and forensic professionals after a review of the crime scenes.

The contention that he happened to take Penny to the woods and find a tree with a noose, already fashioned, seems far-fetched at best. I think that Ruzicka had visited the site before and fantasized about hanging Penny Haddenham long before that day. If we fall back to the excuse that drugs and alcohol were to blame for these murders, we must also look at what was done.

In Nancy Kinghammer's case, his first victim, she was taken to the woods when it was dark. It is hard to see in the dark, for everyone. The darkness did not stop Ruzicka from taking her into a secluded wooded area, so secluded that it took twenty-nine (29) days to find her body. Once there, he strangled and raped Nancy, again, in the dark. Oddly, he went back home to grab a shower curtain from his ex-wife's home to cover up her body in an odd showing of remorse.

This might be the strangest aspect of the first murder, wherein merely leaving the scene would have eliminated almost any evidence against him. Since DNA was not perfected in 1975, there was no way to test if the semen left at both scenes was his. It would have been a non-issue. It was these pieces of evidence (a shower curtain, partial fingerprint, and a kitchen knife) along with his ex-wife's admission to police that Ruzicka was a sex offender who had recently escaped from Western State Hospital. She admitted he had been staying with her. These facts helped to seal his fate once he was arrested for these murders.

In Penny Haddenham's case, she was taken quickly, after beginning to perfect his modus operandi (mode of operating/working), while looking for some material for a dress for her school dance. Ruzicka was learning to take his victims by fear. He knew that some minor small talk was enough to gain just the smallest amount of trust, then he would surprise them with the knife, solidifying control immediately.

Although Penny was found first, she was actually Jim Ruzicka's second murder victim. What is more interesting is the ratcheting of violence and torture he inflicted in such a short period of time. The escalation seen is quite apparent.

Jim Ruzicka goes from walking back to his ex-wife's house (about one-third of a mile or more) to cover up the victim's body in remorse, to openly displaying his victim after hanging her. It is also important to note the level of violence was not only increasing, but his willingness to sexually assault the victim and then to redress his victim post-mortem, shows a willingness to evade the police. If Ruzicka had not been caught, he most certainly would have committed more murders and likely with more torture and violence.

Throughout this interview (both written and oral) we have excuses that substances diminished his capacity to distinguish right from wrong or made it easier to commit the crimes. This is completely and utterly wrong, given what we know about how Penny died. There were semen stains beneath her jacket and her outer clothing. She was raped. She was assaulted. She was scared. For over an hour she was in the presence of a sexual psychopath. Ruzicka wants the reader to believe that all they were doing is cordially talking in the woods until things got out of control. He stated that Penny's throwing of the rope and calling him an "asshole" were what caused her death. Ruzicka, in many ways, blames the victim for her own death.

Of course, Penny was defending herself with all she had to give, knowing full well she was likely going to die.

She knew Ruzicka had brandished a weapon and had already sexually assaulted her. I have no doubt she fought back and called him names after what he did, because he did so without her consent and was likely revolting in how he acted toward her during the ordeal. This was the ultimate fantasy for a "sexual psychopath" with a victim profile of young teenage girls. This was exactly the kind of victim that he would have fantasized about for years. Now, he was alone in the dark woods with her.

It is my belief that Penny likely suffered torture for quite some time. I write these facts regrettably because I feel for her, her family, friends, and loved ones who missed out on everything her life had to offer. This is my assertion given all I know about Ruzicka's past, the facts of her case, pictures of the crime scene, and the autopsy report.

Ruzicka contradicts himself by all that was required to assault Penny. Not only was it necessary to remove her jacket, shirt, and undergarments to sexually assault her but

Ruzicka admitted (after the written interview and through email) that he redressed her after she was killed. We also know this because the forensics tells us this much.

Penny Haddenham could not have had marks on her skin if her clothes were never removed. That is a level of depravity that dismisses the idea that drugs and alcohol played any part in this equation. Someone who was inebriated or had such diminished capacity would not have been able to perform all of the acts necessary to complete this heinous murder. Someone under the heavy influence of drugs would likely have been unable to control his victim for this long without her escaping.

It is also undisputed that she was also burned and bitten, according to autopsy reports. As to what was used and why this was done, Jim Ruzicka denies all of this occurred. This is where Ruzicka tends to show his true motives as a repeat sex offender, blaming substances and even the victims' own words for why they were killed.

Ruzicka redressed a young girl who he had just raped. Then, whether through sheer overpowering of the victim or after strangling her, he fashioned a complex knot around her neck and tied the rope to the base of the tree. The scene was grisly, her jacket showing signs of knife play, torture, and a lengthy battle with a man who was much stronger than she was at merely fifteen years of age.

Penny Haddenham stood no chance of surviving that night in 1974. Ruzicka had already killed a week before and left his victim to the elements. He was perfecting his craft in how he quickly subdued his victims. In many ways, the use of the knife quickly eliminated his victims' ability to scream or shout. His victims quickly learned that he was a sexual predator, grabbing each of them forcefully around the arm or wrist, with very bad intentions. Compliance was not only expected, but it was also necessary for survival.

Jim Ruzicka was deemed a "sexual psychopath" and wrongly sentenced to Western State Hospital. I say that this sentence was wrong because he had already committed several acts of rape, sexual assault, statutory rape, and a host of other charges before being sentenced. What is worse, he was made a trustee. This allowed him to walk out of the hospital. That is precisely what Ruzicka did in January of 1974. Within a month of escaping, he killed two young and innocent girls. The state of Washington is very much to blame for improperly sentencing him and dropping numerous other sexual charges against him. He should have been remanded to prison to serve a life sentence, but instead he was allowed to get into a car and escape.

We know that Jim Ruzicka had a horrific childhood. We know that he was abused, neglected, abandoned, and developed his own feelings of lacking self-worth and learned helplessness because this is what he has stated over and over again.

Ruzicka presents, as many serial killers do, with all four aspects of the *Quadrant Theory of Predictive Violence (abuse, neglect, abandonment, anger/self-hatred)*. These factors led him to develop poor social skills, shape inappropriate forms of human sexuality, and slowly develop the rage that would lead him to kill.

Ruzicka enjoyed sexual assault and rape, we know this because he did it at least six times and had almost no regrets from his other cases. We know his remorse was muted because he continued to do this in various states and may have raped and assaulted dozens of women in his lifetime. Ruzicka was hesitant to talk about his other state cases, although he did admit to two cases in Oregon as well as at least two rapes for which he was never convicted. If it had not been for a brave thirteen-year-old girl in Oregon, Ruzicka may have gone on to kill many more women.

Today, forty-eight years later, Ruzicka has had time to reflect on what he did. He still clings to the idea that he was not of sound mind, but the facts tell us otherwise. If he was not in such frail health, he would surely present a danger to the public if released.

His health issues include two bouts with COVID-19, COPD, high blood pressure, multiple recent surgeries on his hands, falling out of his top bunk which damaged a lumbar disc in his lower back, as well as difficulty breathing. His respirations are heavy, and he struggles to get the right words out at times on the phone.

The important takeaways from this book are that we now know the exact details of the final moments of Nancy Kinghammer and Penny Haddenham's lives. While this might not offer any further comfort to their loved ones and friends, this is the story as told by the last person to see both girls alive. As with the retelling of any story, facts, time, self-preservation, and malingering must also be considered.

Here, the presented crimes are forty-eight years old at the time of this writing. This does not diminish the depravity of Ruzicka's acts, but it would not be unusual for some facts, even if true, to become distorted over time. Ruzicka is still serving his sentence and could be trying to preserve some semblance of responsibility by interjecting the use of alcohol and drugs into each of these cases.

Additionally, we have the killer reliving his crimes, his worst deeds, over and over. Many people are mistaken that serial offenders revel in telling their stories, but this is highly inaccurate. Many times, I have found this can be traumatic for even the most hardened inmate. Ruzicka was candid in my professional opinion, but clearly had avoided some finer details that lead to how and why he was caught. In this book, he admits to suffering from panic attacks and many sleepless nights during the writing of this book. At times he even asked if I would stop my questions, but I continued.

Jim Ruzicka and I will continue to stay in touch. As with all of the inmates I have contacted, the relationship runs its course like any other. Some inmates have called me for more than twenty years, others fall off after a few contacts. Like any relationship, there are many reasons why it does not work out. I do not have time to decipher why, so I will simply move on to the next inmate who is willing to talk to me in a truthful manner. I find that long-term correspondence begets more information than simply asking questions over a few weeks.

To get the full story, or at least the most complete story that can be told, I must continue to immerse myself into their world. I am not saying it is a pleasant world to live in, and I most certainly would not recommend it to anyone. However, I have found that as much as I want to escape it, it has been almost impossible to do so. At this point I have succumbed to the idea that my life was meant to befriend those who are deemed to be "monsters" and to treat them with as much respect as I would anyone else.

If I were to treat every inmate I contacted as a "monster," I am not only doing a disservice to myself, but the human race. If we are to accept that some are born to create and achieve great things, we must also accept that some will grow to become destroyers and do very bad things. They are not "criminals," rather they are human beings who have committed a criminal act. We must separate the two. To define anyone only for their bad acts would be a huge mistake. We must accept that there are many factors that shape all of us.

In the life of Jim Ruzicka, there was far more life before these acts, and five decades of life after these acts to reflect on what was done. In essence, his acts were brief moments in time, they do not define who he is as a human being. The ability to separate that is difficult, but I must be willing to do this if I believe that human beings are not born evil. If I was to believe that human beings are born evil, then I must accept their actions as eventual, even unavoidable.

What I do accept as a clinician, criminologist, and forensic professional, is that we all are shaped by what we see, learn, experience, and feel. It is how each of us interpret and react to these internal and external stimuli that separate us as individuals. For the large majority, we interpret these signals and internalize them, maybe lashing out in some ways, but never to irreparable extremes. For others, for a very small minority of human beings, the lashing out takes the form of severe violence against others.

The psychologically unmet need of a serial killer is what drives them, it compels them to kill and kill until they are caught. The fantasy to kill or hurt others forms at a very early age in life. Eventually that fantasy slowly grows into the need to want to make it reality. When reality comes, and sometimes without much notice – that stimuli makes them feel power. When that power is the ultimate power - choosing whether someone lives or dies – it becomes a compulsion they can no longer ignore. They have become a serial killer.

.

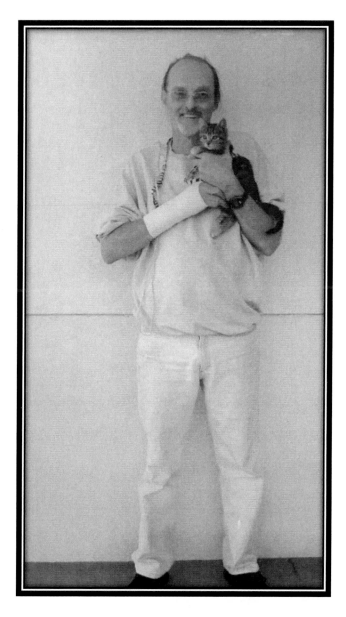

James Edward Ruzicka as he appears today

Folding butterfly card by Jim Ruzicka

The author's handwritten correspondence files from

Ruzicka (2016–Current)

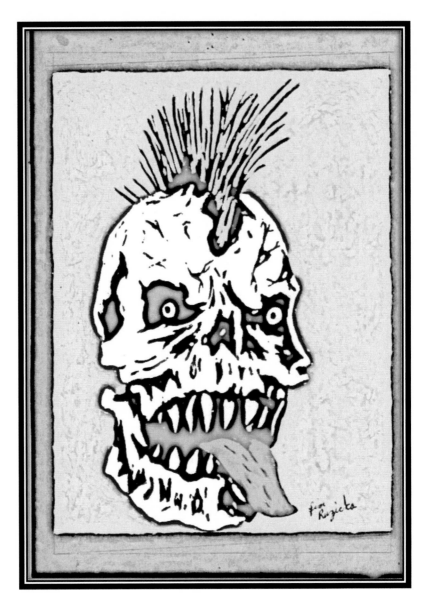

Original artwork by Jim Ruzicka

About the Author

Anthony Meoli has been corresponding with and visiting serial killers for nearly thirty years. He has written to more than 140 serial killers, murderers, white-collar criminals, arsonists, spree shooters, and arsonists worldwide.

Anthony holds a bachelor's degree in criminal justice from Penn State University, a master's degree in forensic psychology from Argosy University, a master's degree in clinical counseling psychology from Argosy University, and a doctor of jurisprudence from John Marshall Law School.

He is a board-certified clinical counselor in Pennsylvania. He worked with sex offenders for six months as a clinician, gaining insight in both large group and individual therapy sessions. This knowledge helped him to better understand the motivations behind the numerous sexual assaults, rapes, and murders committed by Jim Ruzicka.

He currently is employed as a clinical counselor specializing in dual diagnosis patients, primarily with addiction and mental health issues. In addition to his work as a counselor, he consults on media projects and documentaries, and occasionally assists law enforcement or forensic organization with cold case murders or investigations.

Other Books and Interviews by Anthony Meoli

Books

Diary of the D.C. Sniper (co-written with Lee Boyd Malvo)

Forensic Interview of John Orr: The Most Prolific Serial Arsonist of the 20th Century,

Audio Interviews

I Kill for God: Interview with Isaac Zamora (spree shooter)

Interview with the D.C. Sniper, Lee Boyd Malvo

The Bellingham Washington Murders – Interview with the Hillside Strangler, Kenneth Bianchi

Website

www.AnthonyMeoli.net